T0068120

Who Put Ice in My Tea?

Valerie Crowe

ARCHWAY
PUBLISHING

Cover art by Archie Hampton

Archway Publishing books may be ordered through booksellers or by contacting:

Archway Publishing
1663 Liberty Drive
Bloomington, IN 47403
www.archwaypublishing.com
1 (888) 242-5904

Because of the dynamic nature of the Internet, any web addresses or links contained in this book may have changed since publication and may no longer be valid. The views expressed in this work are solely those of the author and do not necessarily reflect the views of the publisher, and the publisher hereby disclaims any responsibility for them.

Any people depicted in stock imagery provided by Thinkstock are models, and such images are being used for illustrative purposes only.
Certain stock imagery © Thinkstock.

ISBN: 978-1-4808-5085-9 (sc)
ISBN: 978-1-4808-5086-6 (e)

Library of Congress Control Number: 2017951753

Print information available on the last page.

Archway Publishing rev. date: 08/11/2017

Contents

Who Put Ice in My Tea?

When I travel, I subconsciously associate certain drinks with places—for instance, in Germany it's beer, in France it's wine (usually fairly classy wine), in Greece it's ouzo, and in the United Kingdom it's tea. Now, to be fair, we in Jolly Old have our fair share of strange drinks, from warm beer (relatively speaking) in the south to IrnBru in the north—and no, I did not forget how to spell. That's how it's written, so get off my case.

Tea in the United Kingdom is obtainable everywhere and is a fine, comfort-delivering hot beverage that is so British as to hardly require further description. We drink tea, from the hot, strong, and sweet liquid guaranteed to start your day off correctly to the delicately scented teas that are served in fine china with the position of the little finger on one hand gently elevated. Imagine the shock to my system when alighting on US soil to be offered tea … *iced!* Shudder. That's just wrong! Surely this was a joke played on unsuspecting travelers from across the pond. When I asked for hot tea, I was brought a mug of merely warm water and an unidentifiable packet of dust with a faint aroma of tea. This was accompanied by a few plastic containers of "half-and-half." Half of what with what? What were they thinking?

Mind you, the waiter had probably never tasted a mug of true "builders' tea." This is real tea—dark, rich, aromatic tea served hot enough to scald your tongue and strong enough to hold up a teaspoon while you salute it. My old grandfather used to drink his builders' tea with two liberal teaspoonfuls of sweetened condensed milk, and if you don't think that would get a wannabe corpse kick-started, then you are sorely mistaken, my friend.

Bear in mind, I was fresh off the plane and just a little weary. All I wanted was a reviving cuppa, but the US of A was obviously oblivious to my needs. They did offer me a variety of substitutes … herbal tea, white tea, jasmine tea, smoked tea (not the illegal type, I might add), scented tea, and … need I go on? But *iced* tea? Really? It was almost enough to make me wonder if I had been just a little hasty in my decision to change my country of residence.

Never let it be said that my stiff upper lip was on the point of trembling—I can compromise with the best of them. I summoned the waiter and through clenched teeth politely asked for an iced tea. In a heartbeat, this large glass filled with ice was put in front of me, and then a jug of some indeterminate brown fluid was poured over the top of the ice. To add insult to injury, a piece of strangled lemon was balanced precariously on the rim of the glass, and a long straw with a paper hat was thrust into this concoction. Packets of artificial sweetener were liberally scattered on the table, and I was left to quench my thirst.

In fear and trepidation, I took a sip through the straw … but nothing happened, probably because I had forgotten to remove the little paper hat adorning it. Now I was not only tired and thirsty but embarrassed too. Eventually, I managed to sip the tea and was overcome with a sense of extreme disappointment.

When in Rome, do as the Romans do, but if you're British, you'd better bring your own tea with you. If iced tea is the only tea-like beverage available, find a pub and order a beer.

Fairy Lights

As a newly relocated British person, I have had to learn that driving over here in the United States can be quite interesting. Yeah, yeah, I know that here you drive on the other side of the road, but it's not that hard to adjust. If the car has the steering wheel, etc., on the right side, you're probably still in Jolly Old, but if it's on the left side, you've probably changed continents at some time recently.

The nomenclature is a whole new language. From a very young age, I was taught that cars have boots, bonnets, and bumpers, while in the United States they have hoods, bonnets, and fenders. (I think I've got that right!) All these changes will cause a Brit to sigh deeply when trying to talk to the repair shop about car problems.

Then there are the number plates! What's that all about? First, in Florida, there are no requirements for front number plates, but one may put some affiliation plate on the front. Whilst one appreciates the fact that some Floridians may well want to advertise their fondness for their favorite schools or sports teams, in some countries (Who mentioned Scotland?) that would be just cause for your car to get egged, and that would be on a good day. As this is a supposed to be a family-oriented article, there is no need to enter into any further description of potential car desecration.

Having dealt with the front of the car, then there's the rear number plate. This is the one that helps the traffic police know where to send your ticket—so I'm told, and we all want to help the police. It's our duty—right? I would not like to hazard a guess as to how many legal styles of number plates are available in Florida alone, but there are more than a few. I've spent more time trying to decide on the style of number plate I wanted than I did when buying my mother-of-the-bride dress. However, I am now the proud owner of a very personalized number plate that I have requested to have buried with me. Might as well; it cost me enough.

Let us now address windows/screens/shields. I have it on the best authority that there is a legal tint level. I have encountered some vehicles that must surely be begging for a ticket, as the windows were tinted so heavily one would need a laser beam to penetrate them. And then we have the gently irritating tint levels on the number plates too. Just dark enough to be a royal pain for those who need to read them, but just light enough to be probably legal. Sigh!

Now we come to the lights. High beams (Are those headlights?), rear lights, reversing lights, fog lights, dashboard lights, emergency lights, parking lights, and fairy lights. I love the fairy lights. They must be for special occasions, such as Christmas, because they are never used for anything to do with driving. What do you mean, they are turn-signal lights? Ha! I know better. I have seen them used for effect during the holidays, but rarely have I encountered them in my neck of the woods being used for indicating a change of direction. I am fully expecting new car models to dispense with them altogether because we all know that they are just optional extras, don't we?

So there I was—toodling along a local infamous highway—when I was astonished to encounter not just one, but three cars using these fairy lights. They could not possibly be turn signals because one car didn't make any turn at all, another was signaling left from the right-hand lane and then promptly turning into a street on the right, and the third car was mine. I was passing a store with illuminated Christmas trees for sale—so I put on my own fairy lights to show solidarity. After all, let's get those fairy lights synchronized, people.

Shopping Carts!
Gotta Love 'Em!

To be fair, it's not the fault of the cart! It's usually the pusher and not the pushee, but most supermarket shopping carts are possessed. Their wheels will lull you into a false state of security as you march briskly into the store armed with shopping list and assorted bags. The first indication that something's rotten in the state of Denmark (sorry, "Hamlet" again) is when you try to make your first turn. Four out of five carts will stubbornly refuse to execute this simple maneuver, resulting in either a hernia for you or a severe traffic problem on aisle three. Firm pushing and a quick kick at the offending wheel will probably get you to the next turn, but by the time you have had to repeat this procedure several times in each aisle, your day is shot.

Another solution is to precede the cart and pull it along. You tend to look fairly stupid, but the shopping day is far from over. Beware of inexperienced shoppers with laden carts behind you. The design of these carts is such that the front wheels seem to be positioned to run into the shopper in front. My heels are scarred from such incidents, and I have been barred from some stores for using offensive language. Well, really! My one and only pair of designer shoes are in intensive care after a run-in (or should I say run-over) with a particularly vicious cart that was being handled by a harassed shopper on a tight schedule.

Then—*shudder*—there is the cart with a peculiar sense of humor. It is usually well-mannered, until it reaches oncoming cart traffic, when it will lurch to one side and get its wheels tangled with the other cart. Warning! Do not attempt to separate the carts with brute force, as the locked wheels will separate when you least expect it, propelling cart and you into a well-stacked shelf of noisy cans, or heaven forbid, containers of something wet and sticky. "Cleanup on aisle six" tells me that the carts have been at it again!

I have a friend who for a short time had to use the *bête noire* of all cart users—the electric shopping cart. This thing had three speeds: a mind-numbingly slow speed (when the produce can't make it to the cashier before its expiration date, it's too slow), a reverse speed that should have qualified for the Indy 500, and a dead stop. My poor friend was last seen exceeding the speed limit on aisle seven, in reverse, while mouthing the words, "Help meeeee!"

She is currently in therapy.

On my last shopping excursion, I saw a shopper who had obviously tried to park her cart in the outdoor space provided in the parking lot, but after having wrestled with it throughout the store, she had tried to teach it a lesson. She manhandled (should that not be womanhandled?) the cart into the parking lot and wedged it firmly between two trees instead. As she turned her back to hobble back to her car (obviously another case of heel-cart trauma), the cart dislodged itself and slowly rolled backward, scraping the side of her car in the process. An accident? I don't think so! It was a case of pure spite on the part of the cart. I have tried to ignore carts and shop using the small plastic baskets, but as my arms now resemble those of a female orangutan, this is no solution. I am resigned. I lurk in the parking lot examining the progress of carts as they come out of the store and try to get a reasonably well-trained one. I speak sweetly to it, gird my loins, and hope that for once, just once, I have found a cart with four functioning wheels and without an attitude. Dream on!

A Real Fixer-Upper!

It has always been somewhat of a dream of mine to buy a quaint little house for a throwaway price, spend some time making it squeaky clean, and just maybe changing a few little things inside. Then I could sell it for a profit. Well, let me tell you that I should have just taken some aspirin and forgotten about the whole idea by the next morning.

For those readers with a death wish, the first clue to the fact that all is not well in the state of Denmark (Shakespeare) is the wildlife. Not just outside, but inside too. I do believe that termites should be Florida's national wildlife symbol, because they are everywhere. If the property is just a bit on the mature side, it's bound to have hosted these special guests at some time. I am learning to look for the telltale signs on the outside in the shape of small piles of termite dust. A piece of supposedly structural wood that closely resembles a piece of chewed meat is a guarantee that this house was on the five-star termite restaurant list, and for all you know, it still is. I know that there is a treatment that involves "tenting," fascinating to observe and scary to even think about. The house resembles a huge wrapped present, and I have the urge to put a large bow on the roof—but then I think of what's going on underneath, and the moment passes. So now the potential profit is receding, and I haven't even started inside.

Bathrooms are really quite simple, but they can be so deceiving. I recommend wearing a pair of high heels and walking over any tiled flooring. You should hear a consistent *clip, clip* as you trot from tile to tile, but if that turns into *clip, clip, thud*, you may be looking at your own personal interior financial sinkhole. The tiles are probably loose at best, and at worst the under-flooring is damp and rotting. Tiled walls that move when you do is yet another invitation to dance around with the bank, and we haven't even set foot in the kitchen. Between the far-from-ideal feng shui placement of the stove/sink/refrigerator hookups, apparently a major factor in kitchen design (I obviously am one of the heathens that never knew this) and the cabinets that list to one side, you have now joined the ranks of the "gotcha" group.

Did I mention windows? No? What was I thinking? Start running, and never, ever come back. If you have a spare dollar to invest for your retirement, buy a lottery ticket. On the good side, there is a sense of "saving a piece of the world" when you embark on any house renovation. It's a bit like surgery. Cut out the bad bits, and help the good bits to stay around longer. If only the Band-Aids weren't so expensive!

Sinkholes!

After listening to local news about sinkholes, I became terrified that Florida was rapidly becoming a piece of Swiss cheese. I sat down (cautiously) and thought about it fairly rationally. It is no wonder that the ground is giving way! Have you taken inventory of the contents of your house recently? I haven't been here long, I have more room than I have ever had in my entire life and then some, and apparently my house is too small! I took stock of just one room and scared myself out of ten years of growth.

On every square inch of shelf space, there was an item that I just had to have as a memento of something or other: an entirely useless piece of glassware, a candlestick, a cute animal figure, a Russian doll set (and they *have* to be all unpacked and lined up, apparently), and even a clay model of the Loch Ness monster! Really? If my shelves are groaning under the weight of all this stuff, what must the house itself be doing? Buckling at the corners and generally trying its best to stay upright! No wonder the ground is giving way … it's just not strong enough to hold everything up. Then there's the dust factor. I know everyone thinks that dust cannot be heavy … after all, it floats around aggravating the socks off everyone and causing nasal passages to swell up and get blocked. But when it settles on all the cute bits and pieces that fill every nook and cranny, it's just got to add to the general weight.

I wonder if it's possible to seal the house, attach a huge vacuum cleaner to a small hole, and turn it onto max. Would that suck out all the dust? Knowing my luck, I would find myself flattened against the wall, hanging on for dear life, while all my china figurines just sat there smiling. And that's another thing. Who was the well-meaning chump who told us to go paperless? It's just not going to happen, people. The proportion of useless mail that my long-suffering mail lady has to stuff into my mailbox most days is unbelievable. Not only are all my shelves filled with junk, but now every other semi-flat surface, table, bed, or chest of drawers is piled high with unwanted papers. Don't tell me to use my recycling bin—I do! But that's the first thing to get filled, usually the day after it has been emptied. So that leaves six more days of shredded stuff to accumulate. My shredder is on overload, and I use more shredder oil than I ever thought possible.

I do not want to hear about closets, either. There is a fine line between being as proud as punch that some clothes still fit after twenty-five years, and sporting myself to all and sundry as a receptacle for out-of-date fashion. Bell bottoms and a hippie shirt! Really? Hot pants? What was I thinking? So there's another hundred or so pounds of useless weight filling just one of my closets. I do try—really, I do. I take stuff to the Goodwill, I put out boxes and boxes for charity pickups, and still the stuff comes in.

When was the last time you checked your attic space? I dread to think of the tons of very special items that have been hidden away in the attic. After all, they were such bargains, etc. Just keep telling yourself that. In a vain attempt to arm myself, should that latest crack in the driveway be an indicator that my house was destined for China, I did make an attempt to weed out some of the antiquated tools that were filling up the garage, but the subsequent insecure feeling that maybe I might need the whatever it was at some time in the future won over the intelligent "Who are we kidding?" And the house groans on!

Soap Dispenser Battles!

I consider myself to be reasonably smart, with an average IQ. However, during the past year, it has come to my attention that Floridians in particular—and probably Americans in general—have a creative bent that is linked to a death wish. If I could find the designer who is responsible for that piece of bathroom hardware, the fitted soap dispenser, my killer instinct would be hard to suppress.

I was lulled into a false sense of security when I moved into my first Florida house. The bathrooms all looked very modern, with stone or granite lookalike countertops and holes drilled through them for installation of said soap dispenser.

My first inkling that there was something not quite playing to the Marquis of Queensbury rules was when the first dispenser was obviously empty. Are they easily accessible? If you are double-jointed and in the first flush of youth, probably. I am not and am not, in that order. When you have crammed yourself into the bathroom cabinet under the sink and said receptacle has been located and unscrewed, no matter how empty it appears to be—it isn't. Drops of whatever was in there before have been waiting for this moment to land on your face or in your mouth, if either is in the direct line of fire.

These receptacles have a life span of about four refills before the plastic threading wears/splits/cracks, never to hold liquids ever again. Not a problem, I foolishly thought, grasping said piece of now useless plastic, climbing out of the cabinet and setting off for a tour of local hardware stores. Can one buy just the plastic container? Of course one can't. However, for vast amounts of your hard-earned cash, they will sell you the whole thing—new. Grumbling to myself, I bought the replacement. Then came the next round of activity. To remove the old piece of now useless hardware, ideally one needs a torch (flashlight) and two pairs of pliers. (I have no idea what the local colloquial term is for pliers, I just know them as pliers.) Next, balance the flashlight between your teeth, grasp the outer ring nut (I don't know what you call that here, either) with one pair of pliers under the washbasin, then extend the unoccupied arm to about five times its length so that, somehow, purchase can be obtained on the upper piece and attempt to loosen the holding nut. It is now necessary to take two weeks off to restore the movement to your damaged rotator cuff.

Let us assume that the offending piece of equipment has been removed! I have been told on very good authority that plugs are available that just slot into the countertop hole that is now waiting to receive earrings/pills/valuable jewelry, etc., from which recovery would entail another foray into the nether regions of the under-the-sink cabinet.

Memo to self: Self! Measure diameter of the new hole accurately. They make thousands of such plugs, and the one you buy will not fit into the hole that has been created.

Trust me on this: I've been there, and will be going there several times again.

So who is this evil genius that thought these fitted soap dispensers were a good idea? His invitation to tea is hereby rescinded.

Thank goodness it's tea time somewhere. I'll invite a plumber.

Double-Wrapped to Keep the Flavor In!

This was supposed to be a serious chapter, but it's no good! I am a victim of the multilayered wrapping and packaging that surrounds just about everything that I have recently bought.

Scenario: My toothbrush was looking a little the worse for wear. It had been with me through a few dental nightmares, and the strain was beginning to take its toll. It had been a good toothbrush, and a friend to me. Maybe using it to get into all the little cracks and crevices in and around the bathroom caused it to splay out a little, but then none of us have totally resisted the aging process. Modern toothbrushes just don't appear to have that "till death do us part" sense of loyalty.

I drifted into the local drug store to buy a replacement toothbrush. Piece of cake, right? Well, one may buy the item, but getting into the packaging is a different kettle of fish—or should I say, set of teeth.

I removed my purchases from the shopping bag and sat down to examine my new toothbrush that was double-wrapped in a simulated see-through plastic coffin. "How hard can this be?" I thought. Pause for hysterical laughter!

I tried opening the coffin-like case with my fingernails, broke several, cursed mightily, and then, to use a phrase taught to me by my military son, fell back to regroup. I paused to file down my broken nails and attach Band-Aids where required and then attacked the casing again, this time with scissors.

Note: Never try this with nail scissors. A machete, maybe, but never nail scissors. First off, they bend. To give them their due, they did make a hole in the non-bubble part of the casing, as well as scoring a two-inch scratch in the granite countertop, but they didn't even make a dent in the main bubble. Now, knowing that my new toothbrush was locked inside this apparently impenetrable casing was causing a dangerous rise in my blood pressure. In fact, I was close to being quite miffed about the whole process.

I tried nibbling and chewing round the edges, remembering the adage that a mother's saliva will act as paint stripper under certain conditions, but I ended up poking a piece of the jagged plastic into my gums. (That's another visit to the dentist—my next thrill for the week.)

Amid my frustration, I dimly remembered reading somewhere that to open up difficult plastic bubble wraps, one should try using a can opener. Are you kidding me? How many of us have can openers hanging around in the bathroom? I just wanted my new toothbrush, but instead I had broken fingernails, Band-Aids on three of my fingers, lacerated gums, bent nail scissors, and a scratched countertop. (Thank goodness I left the machete in the garage!)

I am contemplating buying an electric toothbrush, *but wait!* The replacement heads come in bubble wraps. Get the can opener ready.

For goodness' sake, put on the kettle! It *must* be teatime somewhere.

Colds, Flu, and Other Germs!

They are all at it! They come at me from all directions—in the supermarket, in the movie theater—and to top it off, they seek me out in my own home. Who are they?

They are germs! The germs that carry the insidious sicknesses that can turn even Mr. Muscle into a quivering jelly. Is nowhere safe? (Pause to wash hands while singing the Happy Birthday song through twice!)

My house is littered with disinfectant wipes, and I am considering designing my very own travel outfit using tasteful wipes as part of the accessory list. My shopping bags have their own built-in sanitizer, and I think I should invent a circular shield that fits around my body so that no one can touch me. I recently called my friend who had visited me a few days before, and she answered the phone in a hoarse whisper, liberally interlaced with racking coughs and a few sneezes thrown in for effect.

OMG (to use the colloquial acronym), I am doomed. She visited my house just a few days ago, which means she was well into her incubation period.

Germ alert! Germ alert! (Back to hand washing.) My family and I have mastered the art of attaching disinfectant wipes to our hands during the day, so if we look at, touch, or even think about any inanimate object that just may have become a breeding place for those germs, then we are at the ready. (Wash hands again!)

Forewarned is forewashed in my house. Those sneaky suckers can collect anywhere. Even the backs of necks are not immune. How many times has a close friend thrown his/her arms round your neck during an effusive greeting, not knowing or even caring how many germs may have jumped ship during that PDA? Steam cleaners to the fore! Present mops! Ready, aim, *steam!* Let no flu/cold germ go undetected, and may they perish in the clouds of steam emanating from the magic steam cleaner.

This too shall pass. My consumption of orange juice has quadrupled, and hot toddies have been requested—as purely preventive measures, you understand.

All our toothbrushes have been put through the dishwasher—I am considering running myself through as well, with a hot rinse to follow and maybe a hot finish.

Visitors are requested to present a current health certificate, which will be scrutinized for veracity and accuracy, only accepted after the ritual washing of hands. (Happy birthday to you, etc., etc.) Facemasks are handed out if a sneeze is even being contemplated. I'm thinking of steaming my keyboard, but I'm told this will not improve its ability to function.

Just a cotton pickin' moment! Do I detect a faint tickle at the back of my throat? Time to bring in the heavies! Fluids, vapor rubs, and hot toddies are on standby. Appointments are all canceled! I'll get those germs yet. It will take more than a mere germ to lay me low. Think I'll wash my hands again and again and again, *ad nauseum.* Happy birthday to me, happy birthday to—*cough, hack, sneeze!* I am doomed! Where's my tea?

Is There a Real Person Out There?

As a relative newcomer to the US of A, I find myself reeling from the combative approach that one needs when trying to reach someone with a pulse at the other end of the phone. I have spent many frustrating hours being grilled by a computerized voice that just fails to understand my lack of an American accent. After a fruitless couple of hours spent punching menu buttons and wishing that I could just reach through the phone and unplug whatever it was that kept telling me, "I don't understand you—please repeat the question," I punched every button available to arrive once more at the same place I started.

I tried again, but the computer had my number. It nasally told me, "If this is a complaint, please press one." Or, "Please hold for a customer service representative. Your call is very important to us, so your wait time is forty-five minutes."

By the time you've lasted forty-four minutes, you will be told "We're sorry, the call load is unexpectedly heavy today. Please hang up and call later."

Before you explode in apoplectic rage, let me impart a few words of wisdom. Screaming down the phone at an inanimate but intensely frustrating computer voice will elevate your blood pressure and not bother the voice one iota.

I'll fix you, Ms. Computer Voice! I'm ready to do battle. I understand that somewhere there is a cheat sheet with a list of numbers that are guaranteed to get you to a breathing person, bypassing the voice. These numbers are specific to the company with whom you wish to speak, and the list is worth more than gold dust. I have yet to lay my British hands on this list, and if I ever do locate it, it will be laminated, stored in my bank safety deposit box, and left to my children in my will.

As if the phone system isn't enough to drive me to drink, the voice locked inside my car navigator may well be. I did experience a little difficulty with the heavily accented female voice that was the default, so I changed the settings.

Now the voice and I speak the same language. Introducing George—my very own piece of Jolly Old in my car. We understand each other, George and I. When George tells me to turn left at the next available opportunity, I will happily try to do as I'm told. I have to, because otherwise George will sigh deeply, tell me that now he has to recalculate, and what was I thinking! (That may be just a little bit of literary license, but it's tough out there!) George is probably rolling his eyes at me in his little computerized world, as he has no sense of humor. Once again, screaming at George will do you no earthly good at all. There should be a program that senses your frustration, so that George can gently advise you to calm down before there's a bigger problem. I'm sure that road rage will soon be replaced by navigator rage, and that day is not far off. Cars can already sense when to brake; they can park themselves whether you want to park or not and tell you when not to change lanes. So it's not too much of a stretch for your GPS to sense your mood and tell you to take a chill pill. If you fail to obey, then George might then just refuse to allow you to drive anywhere.

I know when I'm beaten. If you want to sympathize, press one. Want an invitation to tea? Press two. George is not invited!

Mother Nature!

The whole family is delighted. The newest baby is about to arrive any day! The bad news is that every time the phone rings, one turns into a nervous wreck. The fact that the unborn infant is taking her sweet time is just one of the things up with which one has to put. After all, I'm just the grandmother. What is happening is that every acquaintance is casting pitying glances and shaking their heads. If I've heard one horror story, I've heard a thousand. "When I was expecting," followed by "When my children were born (back in the war), they were *sooooo* big that they had no baby beds large enough." It never ends. The next person who greets me with "No baby yet?" is probably going to get short shrift. I have toyed with the idea of wearing an updated bulletin board when I leave the house, as well as putting a stern expression on my face to match.

If it's this bad for me … you can guess what the poor mother is going through. How can any sane person look a forty-weeks-pregnant woman square in the face and ask her if she's had her baby yet? *Really?* What should have been their first clue? The fact that the mother can't get in or out of any seat? Or maybe that she can no longer wear anything that was not made from a large sheet with a piece of elastic holding it in place.

I have heard that there are some women who never look pregnant. They just screw up their face, wince a little, gently cruise to the OB clinic, and give birth while wearing a smile and immaculate make up. Sort of on par with a well known member of the royal family. Stroll in at breakfast, give birth, have your hair done, don one of the latest fashions, to include heels, and go home. Yeah, that'll be right, as they say in Dundee! I'm guessing that in our family this awaited infant will decide to brave the outside world at the most inopportune time, and very probably in the middle of the night, when the mother, the father, the dog, and probably the doctor are ultra-tired already.

She will be a joy at whatever time she arrives, and then we will instantly forget this past week or two. Well, as a grandparent, I will, because I know she is going to make her presence felt from that time onward. So please, trust me—you will know when the baby arrives. I will have a silly look on my face, and I will let you and the rest of the world know, loudly and clearly! Until then, *please* don't ask me. Is that the phone? No, my AC is just fine. Go away!

All Dressed Up and Nowhere to Go!

Where I come from, if you are dressed in your Sunday best and it's only Wednesday, there's only one place you could be going! It's to the doctor's clinic. You would think that on such an occasion, you would be feeling so much like a cat's used furball, that the furthest thing from your mind would be *haute couture*. Well, you'd be wrong. No matter that you consider yourself at death's door—you will make the effort to dig out the new underwear that you have been "saving" in your drawer for emergencies. You will also wear your latest fashionable outfit and try to cover the ghastly pallor of your skin with many layers of makeup. Some will even schedule a hair appointment, too. Trust me on this one!

All of which makes me ask myself: Self! What's that all about? Remember when our mothers would insist that we wear clean underwear when we left the house because "one never knows when one might have an accident"? Strange, because if one did have an accident, the skivvies are likely to be the first casualty.

Even here in sunny Florida, it's possible to keep up with the latest fashions by hanging out at the local clinics. The most dreaded phrase one can hear when making an appointment is, "Please refrain from wearing any makeup or perfume when you attend the clinic."

Are they crazy? Sick or not, there's no need to scare Joe Public by turning up *au naturel.*

None of this withstanding, I dressed very carefully for a recent appointment, even though I felt like yesterday's dinner. I was curled up in the waiting room in a fetal position, still trying to display my designer sandals, as one does, and having a little time before my appointment, I decided to spruce myself up a little. Using a miniature cosmetic mirror about a quarter-inch in diameter, I held it up to my fevered brow so that I could check that at least my eyebrows were conducting themselves accordingly. Then, horror of horrors, I noticed a stray whisker that had just appeared where no self-respecting whisker had any right to grow. As sick as I was, there was no way I would let any doctor peer at my face with that sprout waving around, attracting attention. I frantically scrabbled in my purse, but of course there were no tweezers to be found. I had to resort to the self-plucking method using my fingernails, but to no avail. If anything, the offending hair was getting longer with all the attention it was suddenly receiving. I was mortified.

What to do, what to do? All those out there who have found themselves in a similar predicament will know the answer. I dragged myself out of the chair in the waiting room, crawled up to the receptionist's window with my hand firmly clamped over the offending whisker, and rescheduled. After all, I may be sick, but by golly I'm going to be well groomed while I'm fading away!

Birthdays, Here and There!

As I have recently celebrated a birthday—and no, the actual number is not for publication—I thought I would share some thoughts concerning my past few January celebrations.

Before I made the decisive trip to the United States from Jolly Old, most of my birthdays were highlighted by absolutely rubbish weather. At my somewhat advanced age, I was rapidly becoming used to the fact that "over there" the first item on the agenda would be, "Is it snowing?" This would be followed by, "If it has stopped snowing, has it frozen?" On the odd occasion when none of the white stuff was immediately visible, it was considered a very smart thing to do to check out the garage roof. Many's the time I have looked out of the window, smiled at the rapid thaw underway, and galloped outside with glee. Memo to self: Do not slam the front door. You are likely to be submerged by the mighty avalanche of snow that will descend upon you from the garage roof. This will guarantee to be an anticlimax, whatever your age. The delight in seeing the pure white snow settling gently on roofs, branches, and pavements (sidewalks in US-speak) is very short-lived when every form of transportation is late, stopped, or buried in a snowdrift.

Not to be too depressed, I decided on a relatively recent birthday to get out of Dodge if I wanted to celebrate at all.

One of my more vivid memories is of spending said birthday stuck in an airport hotel because the air traffic controllers somewhere in the heart of Europe were on strike. I wasn't even traveling in that direction, but then, no planes were coming to fly me off to warmer climes, either. I was sorely tempted to have my birthdate changed by deed poll, I can tell you. I was fed up with having to make sacrifices to the weather gods to have even a snowball's chance in the hot place of having acceptable flying weather. When I eventually made it out, the transatlantic journey was fine, but then my ongoing flight was on a teeny tiny plane that I am reasonably sure was built with Lego blocks and rubber bands. There was only room for the pilot, his coffee holder, a map, and his terrified passengers—one of whom was me. A wee man outside this contraption was spraying the wings with deicer and knocking off the sheet ice that had accumulated on the wings during the past four or five seconds while I prayed long and hard to any deity that might be on the same wavelength as me at that time.

Kudos to the pilot—he reached our destination on time, but it took him a good few minutes to pry my fear-frozen fingers away from the back of his seat.

"Enough is enough," I said to myself, and I moved to Florida. So how did I spend this last birthday? A leisurely lunch at the beach, tea that was iced (will they never learn), and a siesta on the warm sand lulled by the gentle breaking of the waves.

The sun was warm, not too hot, and there were no mosquitoes or other irritating biting insects. It was perfect. Any planes droning lazily overhead would certainly not require their nether parts deiced. I can handle this type of birthday. The most dangerous part of the latest celebration was not having a fire extinguisher at the ready when I had to blow out far too many candles. By the way, will the sadistic person who invented the continuous-burn candle please stand up? I am unfriending you forthwith. On the whole, I'll keep my birthdate and just plan to be here and not there for all future celebrations.

Be My Valentine?

I'm sorry; I feel that Valentine's Day is specifically tailored for the beautiful people among us. How many of us have sat waiting for the mail to arrive on February 14 with bated breath in the hope that someone, *anyone*, will have sent us a Valentine? All the cheerleader/quarterback types have a nonchalant attitude as they wade through the myriad of cards from hopefuls, while the less attractive of us would pay to get even one card. It's not important to know the sender; it's just important to be a receiver. Sending out cards just does not give one the same sense of belonging. There were many February 13s during my school days when I spent my allowance on treats for all the less prepossessing of my friends, even the most disliked students in my class, in the vain hope that they might, just might, consider sending me a Valentine card. As you have probably gathered by now, the result was a walloping absence of anything remotely like a card in the mailbox. The only outcome was that all those who were the last person ever to be chosen for anything would suddenly decide that I was their final refuge and sit at my lunch table, or save me a seat next to them on the bus, thus preventing me from ever moving up the social ladder. Serves me right!

Howsomever (I love that phrase), I have yet to sink to the depths of having my pet send Valentine cards to pets of my friends. Bad enough when one's pet gets an invitation to a birthday party of a neighbor's pet. I am living in expectation that Fluffy or Fido will send out invitations listing the pet supply stores where they are registered. Heaven help us when puppy or kitten showers start to be the "in" thing. If one's pet is snubbed by not being included, will one have to watch out for cyber pet bullying next? So come on … 'fess up! How many of you have special email accounts for your pets? You may think I jest, but that time is not far off.

In the meantime, I will smile at the local tradespeople, even the ones who obviously hate their jobs and will take it out on any poor souls who cross their paths, in the vain hope that maybe they want to send me a Valentine. Also, the person who snitched my parking space in the shade (almost a federal offense in Florida) because their car was older and more scratched up than mine (and she was *much* bigger than me) need *not* bother. Her Valentine may have words in it that are not appropriate. Mine to her would certainly not have hearts and flowers.

Blackmailing one's children into sending one a card doesn't count. That could be construed as child abuse, but occasionally, as yet another February 14 comes and goes and all that is in one's mailbox are bills, circulars, and unsolicited mail, the thought does cross one's mind to maybe not want to cough up for this and that demanded item. After all, if one is unloved enough not to warrant a measly Valentine—well, they will just have to suffer the consequences. On the other hand, receiving an anonymous Valentine has a certain thrill level. That is, providing it is not followed up with begging letters. I've had one of those, and they don't count. I will wait for the mail tomorrow, on February 14, in a state of excitement to see if someone out there wants me to be their Valentine. I am not holding my breath!

On Yer Bike!

This is a colloquial street phrase from Scotland, which is sarcastically meant to mean "Buzz off!" However, I am wishing that more people over here in Florida would literally get *off* their bikes. Seriously! Are they looking for a free ride to the ER? I am now convinced that they must come from the planet Krypton and are empowered with super strength and miracle vision, and are able to stop speeding cars with an intense gaze.

For a start, I don't care if you consider yourself a ten in body form, but those padded skin-tight shorts do *nothing* but make the bike seat more comfortable. They certainly do not make me want to rush out and buy myself a pair or three. Then the occasional helmet-wearer ... unless they are competing in some form of speed trial, is it a requirement to have a pointy-head helmet? I think not! However, let us not poke fun at these knights of the road. They are at least out there, burning up a calorie or two and defying every traffic law in the book. Red lights? Must only be for cars, because these cyclists just breeze through them. Give them their due; they do glower at cross traffic, though.

Now let us briefly touch on bike lanes. What are they for? Certainly not for bikes (cyclists, sorry)—maybe they're for parents teaching their offspring how to handle their new bikes, now that the training wheels are off. I have a theory that cyclists like to travel in packs, and they like to chat among themselves. However, these bike lanes are way too narrow for three riders side-by-side. Therefore, let us all pretend we are a car and fill up the usual traffic lanes so that real car drivers behind them can slowly weave back and forth in the vain hope that an opportunity to overtake these wobbling two-wheelers occurs before senility sets in.

My all-time favorite incident occurred when a cyclist of medium age with the inevitable pointy helmet and hysteria-inducing bike shorts was cycling, for once, all by his lonesome in the bike lane. Give him his due—he did stop at the red light. Then he remembered it wasn't really for cyclists, so he sailed blissfully across, causing cross traffic to say very rude words. Just to add insult to injury, after the light turned green, I drove off watching this cyclist ahead of me (still in his bike lane, you understand), and just as I almost got level with him, he turned, stared at me from under his little pointy hat, pedaled across my lane, and made a left turn! Silly me, I was looking at least for some indication that he might be turning … even getting a rude finger would have been better than nothing, but Mr. Oblivious lives to cycle another day!

I am relatively sure that their attitude stems from the tight shorts. Apart from cutting off the circulation to vital areas of one's anatomy, surely one must get fed up with the lack of civility offered to one by the rest of the semi-civilized world. I'm personally surprised that there has not been a cyclist cartoon character created because—let's face it—pointy hats and soprano-making shorts are asking for it. The little dingy bells don't help, either.

If they would just obey the traffic signals, we would look upon them with long-suffering understanding, and I would not need to book a session with my therapist. So on yer bike, O travelers of the open road. May your helmets never pinch, and may the elastic in your shorts never give you a moment's concern.

To Bee or Not to Bee?

Hopefully the Bard will forgive the play on words, but bees are a problem for me. Across the pond, we have huge, fluffy bumblebees that can often be seen flying erratically with enormous bags of pollen attached to their legs. Then there are worker bees that spend time dancing and directing other workers to pollen-rich sites, and then there's the queen! She will reign supreme until she abdicates, dies, or becomes too old to lay eggs—or just wakes up one morning feeling brassed off. Then she will be told to bee off, and off she will buzz away to queen it over some other hive.

It has come to my notice that there are many more species of bees over here—all very confusing. For instance, there are the weird bees (carpenter bees, I think) that bore holes in freshly painted woodwork ... causing me to gnash my teeth in frustration. If that's not enough, there are those little solitary bee-like insects that build mud nests, and who get very annoyed when a well-aimed jet of water indicates that they should relocate. Memo to self: Try not to be really obvious when aiming jet of water onto mud dauber's nest, because they (the bee or whatever it is) will find you very quickly, and the resultant union will not be pleasant for the water aimer.

It is such a shame that I am a honey lover! Local honey, foreign honey, clear honey, cloudy honey, runny honey, and honey that needs to be chipped out of the comb—any honey will find a place to stay in my pantry. So I really need to *bee* alert so that I don't get confused.

Now if I could readily identify the friendly type of bees or bee lookalikes, I would be ahead of the game. Little nests that hang down, usually on sides of windows, are usually inhabited with a type of wasp/bee with a very sour disposition. Someone in authority should tell them that if they built their very clever nests somewhere where humans would be unlikely to even notice them, they would not then be subjected to a lethal jet of whatever the popular wasp/hornet deterrent is. Boy, do they ever get mad! I am considering changing my address, but those suckers would probably follow me. And that's another matter! You would think that two or three cans of spray later, they would catch on to the fact that building clever little nests under the mailbox is going to get them sent to the great hive in the sky, and that would be sooner rather than later, as those critters hurt when they sting.

I count myself lucky that I do not yet need to carry an EpiPen around with me, but if it's all the same to you, I'd rather not have to test my resistance to bee stings at this or any time in the future.

I was always taught that the bigger, cuddly-looking bumblebees will do their honeyed best *not* to sting you, as the action of stinging also removes their inner works, so you may well be stung, but they will have been recalled to join the Great Beekeeper—not in anyone's best interest, really.

Now wasps, for instance, are just mean. They will not only sting and run, they will execute a fly-round and come back and get you again, and again and again! So unfair! So you see, I do have a problem not only with American bees, but also with the wasp, hornet, and whatever else flies with a stinger in its tail. I see no reason to wait for an introduction accompanied by a natural history lesson on bees and wasps, because by the time I have realized that I need to learn the difference, I will have already been stung. So to bee or not to bee, that is the question, and I do not have the answer.

Buzz ... Whine!

'Tis the season! In fact, for most of the year, it's the season! The token insect for Florida has *got* to be the mosquito. They should put their pictures on postage stamps. They seek me out whether I am inside or out. Do I have screens? Of course I do. I have decided that the little suckers (literally) are born with the ability to sneak through the smallest screen mesh, and once inside they lurk until they are big enough to find me. I thought that if I stayed inside, I would be safe, but no! I could be in bed, in the shower, clacking away on the computer, my thoughts elsewhere, when the urge to lazily scratch a hitherto unnoticed itch is the sign that they are *inside!* Again!

I have armed myself with a myriad of solutions to the irritating (of course they're irritating, dummy—they're mosquito bites) bumps and swellings that materialize overnight. I have tried WD-40 (I am assured that a quick blast of this will stop any itching) and smears of Vicks VapoRub. I have ventured outside with sheets of fabric softener stuffed in my pockets, down my shirt, in my sleeves, in fact anywhere that I can attach a sheet, but to no avail. They're everywhere! In fact, I have it on the best information that I am the *plat du jour* for the local mosquitoes, and I'm fed up with it. I am tired of walking around smelling like the inside of a mechanic's garage, or like a locker room oozing menthol fumes. I resemble a scarecrow with flapping pieces of softener sheets blowing in the breeze, and still they find me. I have heard that one solution is to grow a lot of body hair, but I discounted that as being silly! If that really worked, then all the waxing salons would go out of business.

According to my research, albeit somewhat limited, I read somewhere that it's only the female mosquito that bites, and that the males are probably reclining in a hammock lazily scratching themselves or catching up on the local sports news. I would therefore deduce that there must be a declining mosquito population, as it would be the poor ladies that get clobbered/squished/sprayed as they attempt to bring home the bacon, so to speak.

Personally, I know this is not a novel idea, but Noah missed a great chance when he failed to exclude the pair of mosquitos from the ark. Mind you, he probably hadn't been bitten by Mrs. Mosquito—or if he had, he wouldn't have started to itch until they were well into the forty days. Bet he would have been kicking himself later on, as the bumps made themselves known. So I am sure that there is someone out there who is going to tell me about all the good that mosquitoes do! What? Nobody? I suppose that if they didn't distribute diseases through the transfer of blood (yuck), then our researchers would be a bit challenged for something to do! In our dreams, right?

So are mosquitoes the staple diet of anything? Maybe geckos or wee lizards, but those living on my lanai are falling behind with their duties.

I have discovered an aid that is not for the faint-hearted. It does not rely on antihistamines or cortisone creams and sprays, nor does it use the method of spraying one's entire body in vinegar. The critters may not like the taste, but every cat in the area will associate that delectable odor with fish. Well, the cats in Jolly Old would. (Never heard of fish 'n' chips?)

Oh no! The maddening itch can be lessened by applying a cloth soaked in hot water—not just mildly hot, but tea-making hot. If you can get past the potential third-degree burn you could get if you're careless, the itch goes away. Really! The trick is to get it hot enough to make you wish you'd never read that piece of advice, but definitely hotter than a comforting warmth. It does provide relief—not that it helps when you are out and about, but it does help to give you a good night's sleep. Assuming that one of the little suckers hasn't managed to invade the bedding to give you a fresh bite. Is there no privacy?

Snooze, You Lose!

One would think, being retired, that one would have all the time in the world for the finer things in life. The trick is to adjust one's schedule accordingly. In my short time here in Florida, I have tried to familiarize myself with local activities, some of which are proving to be annoyingly elusive. My first act upon retiring was to throw away all my watches and to shut off all alarm clocks. After all, time is not quite so much of the essence as when I was part of several workforces.

That having been documented, I decided to try and get my garden (I do so hate the term backyard—sounds like a prison exercise area behind the Big House!) to be populated with indigenous flora, in the hope that the fauna would follow. To the exclusion of the big ones with teeth and a deceptive lightening turn of speed, I might add. I have planted loads (well, seven) night-scented jasmine at discreet intervals round the outside of the screen enclosure, and these delightful plants have at last decided to cover themselves in glory and subsequent trumpet like flowers. However, the much-desired jasmine scent is working on a very delicate time clock. It seems that between the hours of midnight and zero dark thirty, one may inhale the intoxicating scent of these prolific blooms. Do you see the problem here? This is when I am tucked up in my jammies and sawing logs. I did try to stay up and catch this short-lived occurrence, but as that was in the middle of a tropical storm wannabe, all I could smell was rain. On the upside, when I have guests, I do give them the option of entertaining themselves in the middle of the night to try and experience this wonder of nature.

Turning to yet another case of a plant not working with me, I have a *huge* spiny cactus that is absolutely burgeoning with flower buds. When do they bloom? Apparently it's at dawn! Where am I at dawn? Right! Still in my jammies and still sawing logs.

I once had a friend staying with me who was a very poor sleeper—one of those night prowlers who cannot sleep, raid the refrigerator, and want breakfast at sunrise. They were ecstatic to see this ugly plant absolutely covered with gorgeous white blooms, but there is only about a twenty-minute time frame, and by the time that I had been dragged out of bed, grumbling and rubbing my eyes, the darned things had closed up again! So I guess I am going to have to change my sleeping habits to get my olfactory senses titillated at midnight, and with a bit of luck, I might get to see my cactus blooming. What I want to know is, which insect or bird is it that flies around in the dead of night looking for these wonders of nature? In case they haven't noticed, it's dark out there!

If you're not bored enough reading about these nocturnal horticultural explosions, the star performer has got to be the succulent plant on my lanai that grows pendulous blooms that threaten to snaffle any unwary creature that approaches. I was told that once these *things* look as if they are very ready to do something, I should get up out of my bed at about two in the morning with flashlight in hand and check them out.

I set my alarm and skeptically crept out there, only to be amazed at the stunning beauty of this plant. However, I have to ask the question, who or what was it trying to attract? If I hadn't had advance notice and a very loud alarm clock, I would have missed this whole event. There was not another living thing around. True to fashion, the bloom looked like a chewed tassel by the time the sun came up and normal people were awake.

Who am I to try to understand the God of night-blooming things? Now I really know the meaning behind the phrase, "if you snooze, you lose."

ARCH

Bored? Get a Lawn!

I used to think that grass (the lawn variety) was just that green stuff that grows up between bricks, or on soccer fields and similar locations. I have even seen a lush green lawn that sported a large sign that said "Keep Off the Grass!"

Having acquired a lawn of my own, I now know why the poor lawn owner jealously guards each little blade of grass. It's an art! It is also all-encompassing. Every waking moment is tuned to the health and well-being of the lawn. It has to be watered, mowed, trimmed, fed, and generally coddled. Pests are hurriedly dispatched by carefully controlled pesticides, and the dreaded dollar weed is watched for with suitable alerts sounded should the evil weed be detected.

Now, you would think that with this pampering, I would have the desired plush green lot, but let me tell you that lawn grass is the diva of vegetation. Areas that should be burgeoning with fresh green shoots will cough up a few greenish brown sprouts, thin and straggly, while any lusty grass appears in the center of the flower beds. I have done all that I can. I have taken courses in the art of lawn care; I have fed, mown, and watered as expected; I have even been known to sing to the wretched stuff, but only very early in the morning. I have offered burnt offerings to the green gods and was once seen sitting on my front step with tears of frustration rolling down my face as I surveyed the disaster in front of me.

Not wanting to acknowledge defeat, I went for a walk around my neighborhood, lusting after all the lush lawns that were obviously beyond my capabilities, when I noticed that one frustrated homeowner had ripped up his so-called lawn and had the area paved! An idea was then born in my tortured mind. I took out my cell phone and took photos of this pristine forecourt. Scampering home, I stood in the middle of my so-called wannabe lawn and brandished the photo. "See this?" I snarled. "This is going to be you in a few weeks. I've had it with your temperament. You are going to be like a home run—outta here!" I then started to research costs for lawn replacement.

Now, believe it or not, Mr. Ripley, the next day I noticed that my weedy grass shoots were looking more sprightly and certainly appeared a little greener. Within a couple of weeks, my front lawn was the type of lush carpet that I have always dreamed about, and if I thought I could get away with it, I would erect a "please do not walk on the grass" sign. Maybe I'm a grass whisperer! Maybe I just got lucky, but secretly I know that my grass became afraid—very afraid—and started to cooperate! Anyone for tennis?

Baby Fever

There's a brand new baby in our family. No, not mine, a new grandchild. Now is the appropriate time for the family to realize that the days of having a few spare dollars are long gone. To start with, the modern parent needs an inordinate amount of *stuff*. There are seats for in the car, seats for out of the car, swing seats, special seats for the new mother to nurse the baby, and let's not forget a *huge* chair for the grandmother. Now let us address sleeping arrangements! Cradles for daytime naps, portable swing seats for restless infants, and cribs for nighttime slumbers (who are we kidding).

In between, one should store up what are known (so I'm told) as burp cloths. These are small squares or oblongs of a soft material designed for catching the odd bubble of milk, or even the unexpected passage of some liquid or other from some other orifice. Babies have exquisite timing. Take off the damp diaper, and before you can say "just a minute," there is another exodus of liquid that ruins all your good cleansing work—and probably manages to get the clean diaper too. A three-for-one shot.

Thank goodness for natural breast-feeding. I have been told that there are some cultures somewhere where the grandmother is expected to help nurse the infant. Not in my house, sister! I've forgotten more about that than I care to remember. I'm still working on the origami style of trying to fold a semi-pleated diaper to encase the nether regions of a squirming infant … with marked lack of success so far. Hey! I've done my time in that area. Maybe the art will come back to me in a week or so, but I have torn up my diploma. Now, bath time really scares me. A wriggling live infant covered in soapy water is as slippery as an oiled eel. The parents would not thank me for seeing their newest offspring shoot across the bathroom covered in warm soapy water, because they are really difficult to catch! Trust me on this! Luckily, the infant seems to enjoy the thrill of flying through the air, although my heart rate made it to high aerobic levels.

I will not address clothes—because it makes me cry! Whatever age of baby is on the premises, all the clean clothes are either for the previous age group or the next one. Just believe me when I tell you that laundry is one of the most important skills you will need to have at your fingertips. Plus, baby laundry requires a delicate cleanser and gentle washing and drying. No matter that said baby has covered the wardrobe in various shades of brown, from a soft tan to a very scary chocolate color. There is nothing gentle about that cleansing process.

There is a certain sense of pride when taking the newest member of the family for a walk. Familiarizing yourself with the allocated baby carriage before the first walk is helpful, especially the braking system. I cannot emphasize that enough. I have the scars to prove it. Chasing after the precious gift that has been entrusted to you as the baby carriage revs up speed like a getaway car does wonders for your adrenaline spike. Then ensure that you have mastered the art of adjusting the sunshade/screen to keep the sun out of the face of the hopefully sleeping infant, because in whichever direction you want to go, the sun will take a perverse pleasure in thwarting you. The child will let you know immediately and loudly if the ambient light level is not to their liking. Good idea to practice by yourself when alone. Also, prepare yourself for all the questions that will be thrown at you by utter strangers regarding age and sex of the infant, accompanied by unintelligible baby talk delivered in a sing-song chant by this assortment of hitherto unknown people. If you're lucky, the infant will take umbrage at the resulting lack of baby carriage motion, wail loudly, and scare off these unwanted personages. It is also likely to summon social services unless you are very quick to make your getaway.

It is perfectly true that the second child gets a much more *laissez-faire* upbringing. Washing the hands every few minutes has now been downgraded to … wash your hands when you remember, and preferably before feeding the infant. As that is not my department, thank you very much, my hands stay relatively dry. I am waiting for the day when this baby has grown a little and there is some interaction. Till then, I am going to hide somewhere and take copious naps. Please wake me at tea time, and don't forget to wash your hands!

Going Bananas!

One thing that I love about this area of Florida is that I can now get up close and personal with exotic fruits and plants. I can actually grow my own "mangoes and papayas, everything your heart desires," as the song goes.

Picture this scene! Wandering in my back forty and trying to identify all these strange plants, I found a broad-leafed plant with a pendulous heavy growth, which I now know is the blossom on a banana bush. On closer inspection, dangling above this not-very-attractive cluster of flowers was a "hand" of small green bananas. As I am new to these parts, I had no idea if these were green bananas or plantains. However, the proof of the pudding is in the eating. I checked on the web and learned that one should cut off the flowering growth when it starts to die, then cut the hand of bananas and hang them up somewhere to ripen.

That's where it seemed to get out of hand, if you'll excuse the pun. Those suckers stayed green for ages and also stayed fairly small. I cut one of the fruits, and joy of joys, it was a sweet-tasting banana as I know and love them. What was *not* clear is how in the blue blazes does one then control the ripening so that thirty-six of these don't all ripen or rot at the same time. I'm fairly competent in the kitchen, but my imagination has been taxed to the max with ideas for preserving these fruits. There are only so many banana breads that one can prepare, bake, and freeze, and if I drink one more banana smoothie, I will start to turn yellow myself. This year it has happened again. I am currently walking around yet another hand of smallish but potentially delicious bananas—about forty of the suckers. (Bananas, not hands.)

I am faced with eating/using/baking with maybe ten of these if and when they ripen overnight, and then holding a memorial service for the rest that become overripe and rot before I can figure out what to do with them. My family has eaten their fill, so I guess it's a search for recipes to titillate the palate before I admit defeat. I live in hope that my friends will be able to offer me some expert advice before I go totally bananas.

At the Third Beep ...

My life is controlled by things that go *beep* in the night! They go *beep* even more often during the day too. The beeps are no longer cute—they are downright annoying. Everything electrical that I have bought since leaving Jolly Old beeps, not once, but many times. It beeps when you plug it in, it beeps when you issue a command by pressing a button, and it beeps again when the machine thinks it has completed the mission. If someone doesn't instantly jump to attention and take care of it, it will beep at annoying intervals until a) you switch it off at the source, b) there is a power outage, or more likely c) you throw it across the room until it breaks. I even have a state-of-the-art refrigerator that beeps in stereo. Open the door, it beeps. Leave the door open for longer than three seconds, it beeps again. If you still leave the door open, it cranks up the volume, calls for backup, and lo and behold, stereo beeping in close harmony. Let us not discuss the oven. I have yet to learn how to operate the wretched thing without the detailed instructions in my hand. I am currently able to get the oven to a required temperature, but it's too complicated to try to set the timer. There are just too many combinations of beeps for me to work out what the *beep* is happening.

The security alarm beeps when any door opens, and it will beep when there is any disruption in the program. Memo: If you think you have enough time to deposit the groceries when entering the house before disabling the alarm, you don't. Trust me on this one. You will have to explain to the sheriff why you chose to ignore the alarm, after you have spent several uncomfortable minutes proving your identity. The neighbors get a charge out of that too—nothing like squad cars screeching up to your front door to attract all sorts of attention.

I deliberately disabled the beep on my car because I think it was in league with all the other electrical appliances in the house. It would wait quietly while I pressed the button on the key to lock the doors. I would wait too—then, feeling satisfied that I had outwitted the beep, I would start to walk away. It would wait until I had completely turned my back, and then it would beep as loudly as possible, scaring me out of ten years of growth.

We need a central computerized system at home—a gentle, caring type of computer voice that would politely remind you that your biscuits will burn within the next ten seconds unless you remove them promptly. The voice would gently whisper that the refrigerator works better when the doors are closed, and also that kicking the water boiler would only serve to make it more contrary. A soft, gentle, sort of soothing voice—not these fingernails-on-the-blackboard beeps. I do feel I would respond more calmly to that type of technology. However, should said voice start with the smart comments or give me a general running commentary on how I should or should not run my house, I would be back to the beeps in a heartbeat.

I hear another beep—is my computer battery low? Please let it not be one of the smoke alarm batteries. They are impossible to isolate. The interval between beeps is long enough for you to fall back to sleep, because as we all know, those batteries only start to fail at about 4:00 a.m., just in time to disrupt your REM sleep. When you start to drift off again you are beeped. Many a good night's sleep has been ruined by trying to locate the source of a smoke alarm battery.

Technology! To the fore! This needs fixing. At least get the beeps to beep in the same key! I'm off for a cuppa, if I can sneak in and switch the kettle on before the beeps find me, and it certainly won't be iced!

Weeds!

I know, because my neighbors turn their heads away as they pass, that it's time to weed. My big decision is, what is a weed and what is a flower? I have come to the conclusion that if it grows prolifically, with a root system that reaches down to China, then it has to be a weed. If it cost a month's wages and is so delicate that even a soft spring rain will cause it to give up the ghost (or the root), then it's a flower. So my burning question of the month is, why are weeds absolutely indestructible? You can pull them out, you can burn them, you can swear at them and even pour salt on them ... and a couple of weeks later, there they are again.

I have tried singing to my flowers (probably a mistake), praying over them, feeding them, and generally tending them with a mother's loving care, but they still die. I have discussed this subject with landscapers and gardening friends, and they come up with the weirdest advice. In the blue corner, we have the lack of manure, lack of water, lack of various essential elements in the sand (oops—sorry, soil, forgot I was in Florida), and in the red corner are the group telling me that my sand (soil) is too wet, I am overfeeding the plants, and why don't I throw that packet of Epsom salts away because that's all wrong for this region.

Maybe it's my choice of music! I cannot believe that screaming hip-hop is better suited to coaxing flower growth than a lullaby, because it has stunted any personal growth to which I might have aspired. So, I have come to the conclusion that there is a solution staring me in the gardening gloves. I will allow the wimpy wannabe flowers to go to the great garden in the sky, and I will take a leaf (excuse the pun again) out of John le Carre's spy novels and cultivate the weeds. I will then be able to discard the highly expensive bug killers, the additives, the plant food, and the thousands of bags of weed-resistant mulch. After all, they are just a sop for my vanity. I will have a garden that has *no* recognizable flowers ... just the very prolific, pretty, and seemingly indestructible weeds.

Benefit? I can cancel the landscaping service. The trees will retain their creeping vine clothing—no more ripping and searching for the tap roots of said vines—and I will be left with weed beds that are able to resist anything that's thrown at them. Hurricanes? Not a problem. Drought? No worries. Swarms of locusts? Not an issue. I will lovingly tend my weeds. I will no longer have to continually repair the sprinkler system because my weeds seem to be impervious to hot weather and lack of water, and I will sit back and watch my bank balance revert to normal.

Maybe this idea will catch on. If you are currently the owner of a plant nursery, you may want to find another line of work because I could be onto something big. I hear cries of, "What about the lack of flowers?" All I can say is that I have given the flower thing the old college try, but they are not working with me on this. Former flowers are the horticultural reason that I am almost bankrupt. I have officially withdrawn from the flower race. My worried face scuttling through gardening sections in big stores in the vain hope that I can find a solution to my former gardening problems will never be seen again. That's it! I'm finished! Done! Weeds will reign in my yard. I am going to cut a variegated bunch of no-name weeds as a fetching display for my dining room table. Is there no end to my talents!

Muffins ... on the Table
or on the Hips!

I did it. After a long-overdue scrutiny of my image (fully clothed, I might add), I decided that my muffin top had to go. I tried Aqua Zumba—well, I thought about it, but it was too comical—and I tried the health food route, as I am way too short to tolerate what should be bakery items as a belt. I girded my loins, and my muffin top, and actually signed on at a local gym as well as scheduling sessions with a personal trainer. This was actually less expensive than nuts and bird seeds, as I learned to my credit card's disgust.

I must have had a rush of blood to the head, or all my oxygen was feeding my very own muffin, as I rashly promised a before and after photograph to document my progress. That was my first mistake. The second was to rashly document measurements that I would rather not publish. I mean, really, who is interested in my thigh circumference? Apparently I should have been—interested, that is—for a long time. Then, just maybe, that measurement wouldn't have been quite so large. However, I digress.

My trainer is obviously on leave from some boot camp, as I have stretched, lifted, pulled, raised, and almost dropped more pieces of equipment in the last month than I thought was possible. One does feel a sense of satisfaction at the end of a session when there are aches attached to parts of one's body that are completely alien to exercise. This rapidly moves to the next level about twenty-four hours later. I had the delightful experience of waking up and getting out of bed—well, part of me did. The rest refused to move. I spent time later that day standing through an entire meeting because it was just too hard to sit down and then have to get up again. On the bright side, my muffin top is toned. Yes, I still have it, but it is no longer wobbly—it is now a firm structure. Now I have to get it to move to someone else's waist. As my trainer said, "It took years to acquire it, so don't think it will disappear overnight." Fair enough!

Now, if I can just keep my fat fingers from picking up all the delectable food that's around and putting said food into my mouth, I'll be on a winner. If you want to scare yourself, try doing a calorie count for a couple of days. (Note: A plate of freshly baked chips and an exquisite creamy cheese dipping sauce will have enough calories for a five-foot-two Brit for a whole day—and some.) Quite eye-opening. Did you know that those delicious tiny herb-and-garlic crackers are not too bad *if* you can stop at eating one serving? I think that's a total of five crackers. I waste more than that in crumbs. My new rule is *sampling*. My muffin top cries out for more, but I'm made of sterner stuff, let me tell you. We Brits don't only have a stiff upper lip; we have steely reserve too.

Wait … is that a fudge doughnut? Newly baked? Get thee behind me, Satan … and you too, O doughnut baker. Man (or woman) cannot live by tea alone, so anyone want a muffin?

Fit for Purpose!

I am a theoretical fitness freak. This means that I spend a lot of time researching methods concerning my personal fitness goals, and I collect courses that promise to help me achieve them. There are courses that tell me that I eat too much/too little/incorrectly, courses to keep me flexible enough so that I will be able to write checks to pay for them, and courses to help stave off dementia. What was I writing about? Oh, yes … fitness.

Not that I actually *take* these courses, you understand, but I do think about them a lot, and when the mood takes me I occasionally sign up for them, too. One of my more recent expeditions into considering physical activity was Aqua Zumba. I am not sure that term isn't an oxymoron, but I thought I would gear up for a trial period.

Why pay to go to a comedy club? Just go and visit your local pool, pull up a chair, order a drink, and prepare to be entertained. I considered this form of exercise because most of the body parts that are not for public viewing should be under water. Right? Not necessarily so. The courses are usually conducted in the shallow end to prevent those of us with built-in life preservers from floating off into the sunset, and the instructor needs to be able to see which bits are jiggling uncontrollably so that the exercises can be tailored accordingly. To check to see if you need to take some form of exercise, the rule of thumb is to stand in front of a mirror, naked as a jaybird. (I've never understood that phrase, but I'm assured that most others will.) If your reflection appears to be wearing some form of inflatable fat suit, then it's time to take action. I *did* notice that I had my very own water wings built in, and they are pretty good at keeping me cool if I wave my arms around fast enough to move air currents. Having forced myself into a "form controlling" swimsuit, I discovered that it cut off my breath if I made any untoward movement, so I decided that that form of exercise could be injurious to my well-being. Good-bye, Aqua Zumba.

Moving right along, I decided to attack this fitness topic from another angle. I was going to eat healthily. Armed with enthusiasm, I marched along to one of those places that resemble pet stores because of the inordinate amount and variety of seeds, grasses, and pulses that are for sale. For the uninitiated, pulses are those vegetables such as beans that purport to be good for you, but really challenge your cooking skills after a day or three. They are very good at promoting explosive expulsion of air through one's body, too.

I had my shopping list in hand and rushed through the store, exclaiming at the strange and exotic items available. I mean, really! Hemp hearts? I had to have some of those on principle. Most of the items are stored in huge bins with self-dispensing tubes. A word of caution: Control yourself when pushing the buttons! These miraculously healthy grains, seeds, and the like will pour, and I do mean *pour*, out of the tube into your little bag.

If you are smart, which I wasn't, you will have labeled your bag before the great avalanche of goodness filled it, because as sure as birth, death, and taxes, you will forget what it is when you get to the checkout. They all look alike to the uninitiated, which I was. However, my biggest shock was to come.

I smugly offloaded my purchases to be dutifully weighed and dangled a twenty-dollar bill in front of the cashier. After all, I asked myself, how much can a few bags of bird seed cost? "Is that a deposit?" asked the cashier. A warning siren was going off in my head, screaming, "Run away, run away," but too late! I had managed to run up such a bill that my credit card was hanging on for dear life in my wallet, but there was no avoiding the payment. I tottered out with heavy hemp hearts and more seeds and grains than I knew existed for humans to eat. I am now the owner of a very delicious and expensive granola-like mixture, which I am willing to dispense for just a few dollars per teaspoon. I kid you not. So now I know that I am not rich enough to be healthy. Put the kettle on; it's tea time. May I tempt you with a roasted hemp heart?

'Tis the Season!

They're everywhere! Signs, posters, billboards, from flashing electronic marquees to hastily scribbled signs on pieces of poster board. What are they all touting? "Yard Sale," "Garage Sale," or, for the larger and more grandiose, "Estate Sale."

I am in my very own piece of heaven. You have to understand that this type of event is not very common in Jolly Old, from whence I hail, other than the smaller "Car Boot" variety. (Remember, a car boot is just our name for a trunk.) It does not take much of a stretch of the imagination to realize that there is only so much stuff that can be loaded into your car trunk, but exponentially, almost your whole house contents could be up for grabs in a yard sale.

To make these sales stand out from the mundane, you will notice that they often have catchy names: "Junk from the Trunk," "Whale of a Sale," "My Trash, Your Treasure," and for expats there is always the "Loot from the Boot." I personally think that "A Taste of Money" is a little crude, whereas "Finders Keepers" seems to hint at buried treasure. "Yard Sale" doesn't have that *je ne sais quoi*, but it still brings in the bargain hunters galore.

Now, there are unwritten rules that have to be obeyed. I have learned from bitter experience that if the sale has been advertised to start at 8:00 a.m., you had better be up and fighting fit at zero dark hundred, because the more experienced sale-goer will be beating on your door while you are still in your jammies. These seasoned buyers will have covered most of the local sales before you have even said "Good morning," and if you want to sell your wares, you have to be more than just on the ball.

Another thing to remember: If buyers don't see a specific item for which they have been combing the local sales, they will ask if you have whatever it is they are seeking. It is very uncool to ask them to hold on while you rush inside, pry said object out of the clutching hands of an unwary teenager or spouse or, yes, I'm ashamed to say, even a toddler, and offer it for a dollar even though said object was almost brand new and fresh from the store, where you had spent a week's pay in obtaining it. Your family will not thank you for this. In fact, they may well be a trifle miffed.

Then there are the dealers! You have to play the game, or it's no fun. Many a lively riposte can be heard as they offer to "take all this off your hands" to save you the trouble of sitting in your yard/garage/car all day. That's too easy! The cut and thrust of marketing strategy will bring a sparkle to your eyes and put a spring in your step. Just think! You may have outmaneuvered a dealer who has just offered a quarter for a perfectly good set of lawn chairs, but hard-nosed salesperson that you are, you managed to get forty-five cents. The trick is to only offer for sale things that you really do *not* want anymore. A dead killer is for you to price something at three-fourths of the original cost. That's no fun. Anyone with a little time and a computer can buy that object brand new on sale somewhere. So, learn to play the game.

Now if you are a buyer, there are rules for you too. Do *not* buy stuff that you do not want or need. I can hear it now … "This would be so cute on my bedside cabinet/side table/front porch, and they only want $1.50. That is such a bargain!" Paying by check or credit card is a bit of a no-no too! However, experience is the best teacher. I have come home staggering under the weight of my yard sale purchases, very pleased with myself, only to find that I had neither the room nor the inclination to house these objects after all. But what the heck ... I only spent $4.50.

The weekend is almost upon us. Yard sale boards are blooming in the early morning mist, so get yourself fighting fit and sally forth to do battle. Not a good idea to go to these sales in your designer outfit or the new Mercedes, either. (Assuming you are one of the very few people in the United States who can afford not only to own said car, but also to run it.) Nothing raises prices like a gleaming mode of expensive transportation. Best thing is to borrow the beaten-up truck from an impoverished member of the family so that any extra kicks, scratches, or dents will go unnoticed. Should you be successful in obtaining what is (to you) obviously a valuable antique hat stand or a Chippendale chair for just a few pennies, this transaction will more likely go unnoticed if you heave your acquisitions into the bed of said dilapidated truck. In that case, you are obviously a discerning buyer, so would you please take this as a personal invitation to attend any or all such sales that I will host in the future? I am sure that I have some very valuable pieces of whatever you are looking for—if the legs don't fall off first.

'Tis the season, and I am in yard sale heaven once again.

The Smallest Room
in the House!

I travel a lot—really, I do—to different states, countries and continents, but I would appreciate finding a dummies' guide to operating the various *facilities* available to visitors. Let's face it—or, for the females of the species, let's back up to it, for some of these porcelain objects are a bit of a challenge. Having been born and brought up in the war-torn forties, I hesitate to criticize, especially as I know I'm lucky to even have indoor plumbing, but they should provide operating manuals for users unfamiliar with the version available.

To start with, I have had to learn that it's not too polite in the United States to ask for the loo—rather, one should request to use the bathroom. Doesn't matter that bathing is not on one's immediate priority list; that's how most people refer to the smallest room in the house.

I had the dubious pleasure some years ago of visiting a magnificent bathroom setup that was so ornate and comfortable, I almost expected to have sherry and hors d'oeuvres served while I was visiting. Glistening countertops, gentle but direct lighting, elevator music to soothe the soul, an array of exquisite hand soaps and scented towels, and an attendant to polish or warm the seat— all these to attract the visitor. I would like to divulge the location, but then there would be too many queuing up to visit, and it would no longer be my secret. There are a number (excuse the pun) of receptacles in some places of respite that are so delicately disguised that they are hard to locate among the frills and furbelows. This can lead to rather frantic ripping off of crocheted covers before one may relax.

I suppose that I am going to have to mention airport loos. I think that somewhere, someone is spending time thinking up new and complicated ways of flushing. I have spent many a frustrated few minutes trying to find out whether to push or pull the various chrome contraptions, only to find that it works all by itself. Quite disconcerting when one doesn't expect it, I can tell you. Then there are the revolving seats! Really? Or the lined seats—now that's worrying. I also have a quarrel with those huge toilet tissue dispensers that always look full, but one can never find the end. I wonder what design genius thought of that idea.

We are truly spoiled these days. I remember visiting a public facility in Prague many years ago; it was pristine, very clinical, and guarded by an attendant who was obviously a frustrated prison wardress. I was issued two small squares of toilet paper with an expression that dared me to ask for extra. Two squares? Really? That wouldn't even blot my lipstick. (Luckily, I had a pack of facial tissues with me, just in case.) I have memories of outhouses and rooms that might just as well have been outside, as they were so cold that it was a toss-up whether one would be frozen in position for the duration, or until the next thaw. The visits to foreign parts and those loos that require careful positioning of the feet before business can be attended to (again, no pun intended) are nightmares from which I have only just recovered. Skinny jeans would have defeated me entirely.

Moving on, I simply must mention a visit I made to a Scottish coastal town that boasted public toilets for men that warranted being mentioned in the tourist handout. All the tubing was of highly polished brass, and the tiling was magnificent. The windows sported stained glass, and the *pièce de résistance* was the array of clear glass cisterns. The curator was so proud of this facility that he gave tours—but only when the "rooms" were not busy. He did say that they kept goldfish in the cisterns at one time, but I suspect that his tongue was firmly in his cheek. Interestingly, the ladies' facility bordered on the mundane and utilitarian, to say the least. But I digress. All I ask is that if weird plumbing is installed, please supply a manual! Or a *womanual,* for the technically challenged among us.

Legal Speak!

When was the last time that you actually had a conversation with a lawyer that wasn't totally one-sided? Do they go to school to learn how to be confusing? I've tried getting lawyers to put their thoughts (hysterical laughter) down on paper, so that I could take my time to read through and understand the content, but that was not my smartest idea. While we're on the subject, forget printing out their emails. There are trees in the rainforest that are shaking in their roots because of the amount of paper being used just to try to get a handle on what the blue blazes these lawyers mean.

I know, I know, we are supposed to be conserving paper—but sometimes, it's just not possible to spend the time in front of the computer trying to comprehend the legal content your lawyer has sent. It's best to print out the quire of paper, arm yourself with a stiff drink or three, and go somewhere quiet where you are unlikely to be disturbed. I might add that I still end up totally confused. You have to hand it to them. They have it down to a fine art! I have given it a good deal of thought lately, and I have decided that it's all to do with billing. A lawyer cannot in all good conscience bill you for an hour's consultation (albeit by phone) if the question was answered in a couple of very short sentences that took you about two minutes to read.

However, lawyers have the ability to dress up the answer by first asking the client to repeat the question, then spending the next forty-five minutes quoting similar cases, never answering the client's question, and then slapping them with a bill for an hour's consult. I am so in the wrong job!

While I am in the mood for railing on about lawyers, the actual language they use is about as comprehensive as Swahili to me. Whether we discount the whereas, wherefore, party of the first part, party of the second part, with a liberal sprinkling of hitherto, etc., I am convinced that their language would make much more sense if all this gobbledygook was erased. All they really need is a few succinct sentences, such as: "Yes, you have a case!" "No, you don't have a case!" "I can get you a reasonable settlement!" "You are wasting my time and yours!" and the most important one-liner, "You owe us x amount of dollars." Is that too much to ask? Maybe we would then not be quite such a litigious society. Maybe then we wouldn't need so many lawyers. Maybe then legal advice would be easy to understand and—mercy me—affordable.

What do I know? I'm not a lawyer! I have never learned to speak their language. Now, if a "learn to speak lawyer" language course was published, maybe—just maybe—I would be able to understand them. I am not holding my breath on this one. Time for a cuppa. Now, *that's* understandable.

Form Phobia!

Please don't send me another form to fill out! It renders me a quivering wreck, and I will spend my days creeping around in a fit of despair just in case I've filled out the latest form incorrectly. One cannot avoid it. They're everywhere! Even on repeat visits to any medical office, one is required to fill out forms every time one steps inside the door. I visited one establishment that had a threatening statement printed above the reception desk, which says in bold script, "Do not just declare same information as last time—or your appointment will be canceled." What? Are they serious? Suppose I can't remember what I put down before; did I put down my height and weight correctly? Maybe I grew a bit. Did I lose a pound or two? Is all the information about my previous visit correct? I can't remember, and sure as taxes, I will not be given a copy of my previous form for comparison.

Let us not forget the form given to air travelers—while they are actually in flight, I might add—that asks the question, "Have you been engaged in any terrorist activities?" Seriously? Isn't it a bit late to ask that question when the plane is probably over the ocean? If anyone should be bold or stupid enough to reply yes, what exactly is the protocol from then on? Issue parachutes to every other traveler and plainly ignore the idiot who thought it would be amusing to tick the yes box?

I am reminded of enrollment time every school year. Same school, same teachers, same students, and same parents, but we all, to a man or woman, have had to fill out the same form every year. No option to get creative—and wouldn't it be so much easier if there was box that stated, "If you have any changes to your filed information, please fill out the additional form"? I'd go along with that.

I dream about a utopian society where one's information regarding basic family details is recorded once. Thereafter, one would only be required to fill out a form if changes have occurred. All official organizations would then access this information (after proper clearance, you understand), and there would be less chance of me in particular, and Joe Public in general, making an error and worrying about the consequences.

I even have to fill out forms to receive regular trash pickup, to be able to donate to a charity, and to be able to cancel an order online. That's a good few forms, right there: one form for identification, one to state the problem, and one to ensure that I really meant it when I tried to cancel the order. Nobody who hasn't yet lost the will to live would go through this hassle if they could possibly avoid it. I forgot to mention that they will send me another form to see if the action taken met with satisfaction.

I have realized that there are those among us who wear out shoes, sports equipment, and even cars. I, gentle reader, wear out keyboards filling in forms. Yes, I know that there's a program that will fill out forms for me, but I have to fill out a form first, and then maybe, just maybe, I worry about ID theft, and I might decide to erase this program. Good luck with that. It's all too much for me. Wouldn't you think in this age of technology that the Establishment could just scan my retina and be done with all these forms? And what's up with this electronic signature? Is there a miniature R2-D2 or a C-3PO somewhere forging my signature on demand? Very creepy.

There are no prizes for recognizing that I am way too phobic (Is that a word?) to fill out my tax return. It's almost as scary as shredding old forms that I have saved since last century. (Wanted to say that since 2001, and now I've said it.) I do try to get my information right, honestly I do, but I begin to worry that I've made an incorrect declaration somewhere along the line, and I'd be spending too much time worrying. It is so worth paying a professional to take that risk for me. Turbo Tax? Filling out tax forms all by myself? Online? I should cocoa! Are you serious? They would send little men with special white coats with long sleeves to take me away, and I'd let them, except there's a form to fill out first!

I bet the Queen doesn't have to fill out forms. I can see it now, a little person with a black briefcase with the title "Form Filler, by appointment to her Royal Majesty, Queen Elizabeth 11."

Contrariwise!

Why is it that, when faced with a normal day-to-day situation, I have an impish urge to do the exact opposite of what is expected? Why else would I want to go up a down escalator, or what is worse, secretly hit the stop button for an escalator full of people and see how long it takes for anyone to notice it's no longer moving? What is wrong with me? How many times have I deliberately stepped on a lawn that displays "Keep off the grass" signs? Too often.

After a tedious hunt for my car in a huge car park one day, I drove out past the parking attendant, who in a friendly manner remarked, "Did you find your car then?" What imp on my shoulder made me reply, "No, but this one is a much nicer color!" I am just asking for the label "smart aleck" to be stuck to the back of my shirt someday!

I'm sure that everyone must have this urge to some extent—surely it can't just be me. After all, a sedate Brit of mature age is supposed to be in full control of herself. (I am ignoring the sniggers from family members.) I am actually convinced that this is a national trait. The urge to see the ridiculous side to a lot of the pompous statements that are often printed out on public notices brings out the wicked side of many Brits. How does one not laugh at the sign on an emergency exit that states "This door is alarmed!"

Poor thing … who frightened it? Do the powers that be even read these signs? I am not even going to mention the effect that revolving doors have upon me. Why would I have the urge to go round a few times before emerging? How many of you have pressed *all* the buttons outside an apartment block just to see how many people will buzz you in? Never? Why do I not believe you?

Then there are long, shiny, curved wooden stair banisters. Who, gentle readers, has not longed to slide down a highly polished banister to gracefully alight at the bottom unruffled and splinter-free? At least that can only be accomplished if there are no protrusions or curved figurines to impede one's descent. Best to do a complete recce beforehand. Trust me on this one! Nothing worse than embarking on the slide of one's life, only to find out too late that the curved railing has been embellished with a very painful array of ornate knobs that only become visible as the rail makes a ninety-degree turn halfway down. So, do your homework. Run up and down a few times beforehand to check for splinter possibilities and other potential hazards.

I am trying to curb this side of my personality—really, I am. But then, life is so serious; we have to lighten up a little. There are enough things to worry us during our short stay on this earth, so enjoy it. If you want to run down an up escalator and you are nimble enough, go for it!

Make sure you are quite fit before you try it the other way around, though, else you may need a spare lung when you make it to the top, and you will not have enough breath to blow on your tea to cool it.

Houseboats!

I think I might like to live on a houseboat. Just think! It would be totally away from people, with no garden to maintain and very little housework to take up my time. Okay, so I would need to have barnacles scraped off the bottom every so often, but I can swab down the decks with the best of the other swashbuckling boat people. No more would I toss and turn at night waiting for sleep; instead, I would be rocked to sleep by the gentle motion of the water.

I would not need to fill closets with clothes for every season; instead, I would own a couple of pairs of pirate-like pants and a few flowing shirts. I would be carefree and could discard all of my rewards cards that entice me to spend, spend, spend, because I would no longer have a place to put the purchases. I would become a fish-eating vegetarian (Is there such a thing?), and I would become so healthy that the natives would point me out as an example of a reborn human being. Visitors would be limited to one at a time because I would have no space to entertain more than one, and I and my visitor would be often found sitting on deck, watching the sunset and spinning yarns! (I've always wanted to spin a yarn! Can one wear it afterward?)

My source of entertainment would be watching the world racing by, everyone very busy going somewhere to do something very important. I could smugly lean on the rail of my houseboat and remember the days when I was one of them. I would call my houseboat *Utopia*, and I would be the proud owner of two mugs, two plates, two glasses, and a couple of sets of silverware: one set for me, and one for the occasional visitor. My houseboat should be moored (See! I'm already learning the language of the boat people!) close to a library, so that I would no longer have the urge to buy every book ever written—and some twice because I had forgotten that I already had a copy.

Okay … this is the dream that I have whenever I feel that there are too many people in my actual world. As much as I love them all beyond reason, there comes a time when closing my eyes and wishing I was on my very own secret houseboat is my escape. Now, back to reality—just how stable are these boats? Am I going to need a substantial source of motion sickness pills? Will I start to exude my own special aroma that is a cross between bilge oil and fish? How hot is it likely to get below deck in our Florida summer? Will I be able to sleep on deck without every mosquito on God's acre taking this as a personal dinner invitation? (Me being the entree!) Where will I empty my trash? Would I have a floating trash removal service? I fear not! What do you mean, my cell phone won't work below deck? I need to call my Internet provider because I have bought a new program called Portholes 7 (houseboat speak for one of the more popular computer programs, Windows 7), and it's not working. I have barnacles on my router—now *that's* painful—and the coastguard keeps pointing out the *Utopia* as a "prime example of how not to do boat things." Much more of their sauce, and I'll run the pirate flag (skull and crossbones) up the flagpole. Wait! I don't have a flagpole. Come to think of it, I don't have a pirate flag, either. OMG, there is a hurricane warning. That's it! Houseboat for sale—anyone?

Trick or Treat?

See, we just don't have the same enthusiasm for trick-or-treating in Jolly Old England. Mind you, with communication through Facebook and Twitter telling everyone not old enough for Social Security how to get free candy, it's catching on quite rapidly. Personally, I think it's a ploy by dentists to help drum up business, judging by the sheer volume of lollipops, chocolate, and all sweet stuff in between that landed in my grandchildren's pumpkin baskets. These kids could be on a sugar high for months. There is a fine line between rationing out the goodies and being a real killjoy, so I have found that in order to prevent the kids from having the candy version of delirium tremens, it's easier to eat the stuff myself. I have rationalized this to myself as saving little teeth from decay, but I live in fear and trembling of being caught with my hand in the pumpkin, so to speak.

Here in the sunshine state, it is much easier to participate. The child in cute costume rings doorbell, holds out receptacle, lisps the well-known phrase "Trick or treat," and vast amounts of the sweet stuff cascades into the basket. Most participating families actually make quite a party out of the whole event. Chairs are placed in driveways, and huge cauldrons of goodies are ready to be dished out to visiting vampires, superheroes, ninjas, and a goodly percentage of princesses. The downside is that if one is a chaperone, the most you are likely to get is a number of free mosquito bites. I would recommend wearing a protective costume with lots of flowing skirts or some suit of armor, as the witching hour is also the time when the local beasties have a feeding frenzy.

I suppose the reason this event fails somewhat in the mother country is that the weather is not of the most clement at the end of October (nor many other months). It is hard to keep cheerful during the schlepp round the neighborhood when rain is dripping down the neck of your Mary Poppins costume, umbrella notwithstanding, while a small person is trying to keep the rain out of the candy basket.

I have to find out what happens if the giver decides to push the envelope, or candy wrapper, so to speak! What would happen if, instead of a treat, the homeowner called their bluff and said "trick"? On second thoughts, have you seen the size of some of the kids? Or come to that, some of the chaperones? Personally, I think I should just stick to coughing up a variety of candy.

Hats off to all those kids who are entrepreneurs of the future. Candy baskets? I don't think so. These days, many kids use large trash can liners or pillowcases. No wonder the chaperones ride round the district on golf carts—the sheer tonnage of candy received by any one goblin or equivalent requires heavy-duty transportation. It's enough to make dentists lick their lips ... and that's not because they can taste the candy, either.

Snakes 'n' Stuff!

We all know that some people seem to be smarter than others, so I guess it shouldn't come as any big surprise that some snakes should be smarter than other snakes.

Whilst relaxing on my lanai, I saw what appeared to be a piece of black tubing hitting against the mesh of the enclosure. When I looked more closely, I saw what was obviously a demented black garden snake trying to shred itself through the mesh to get outside the enclosure with zero chance of success. Said snake was of a goodly size. When it comes to snakes, there are small ones and then there are "call somebody to deal with this" ones. This one was not very big in circumference, but it certainly would extend way beyond a 12" ruler. Donning a pair of thick gloves, I bravely decided to relocate this obviously stupid snake.

Having caught it with minimal damage to me, the gloves, or the snake, I went through the lanai gate so that I could return it to the garden environment and we could all be happy. I dropped the snake on the grass, expecting it to slither off into the bushes, but no! It did an about-face, nipping through my feet, and made like Houdini down the nearest drain. "Rather you than me," I said to its tail end and went back inside the screened enclosure. It wasn't an hour later when this snake reappeared back inside the lanai and made a beeline (or a snake line) for the same piece of screen, only to repeat the whole process! I can only assume that the snake had belted through the ground-level drainage system, once again coming up outside the lanai, had maybe managed to flatten itself under the screen door to get back inside, only to repeat the whole process of trying to make like a piece of string cheese at the same place as before.

I can hear the dissidents right now: "How do you know it was the same snake?" Well, I didn't check its passport photo, but it was about the same size and girth as the former dipstick snake, and this one wasn't overendowed with smart cells either. This time, the snake was removed and probably had its internal GPS altered when it was unceremoniously lobbed over the fence into the semi-wilderness back there. Now I have stared at this corner of the screen enclosure to try and fathom what was so fascinating that this snake would twice try to force its way through the mesh! It must have been the same snake—surely there can't be two of them that are so lacking in smarts! So far, so good, but whatever the attraction was outside the corner of my lanai, I'd rather the snakes kept quiet about it.

Economics: A Very Touchy subject!

I have never professed to understand the ins and outs of economics, and taking a college course in this subject just proved to me that I should leave it the heck alone. All those supply and demand graphs looked good on paper, but the whole concept seemed to me to be a master plan for a type of legal fraud.

Take the very American holiday known as Thanksgiving. For weeks before, the price of gas (petrol, to us Limeys) had been slowly sinking, to our great delight. Then the great Thanksgiving shopping hype and family visits began, and for just a few days around the fourth Thursday in November, the price of gas skyrocketed. It's supply and demand, I was told. Then explain to me why this concept doesn't apply to other commodities that are time/date sensitive! Why doesn't coffee cost more in the mornings? That's when more coffee is consumed.

To be fair, the same system applies to hotel rooms. When a hotel room is available most of the year for x dollars a night (just an arbitrary figure), why does the same room cost double or even triple because some well-known people are clouting a wee white ball around on some very nicely mown grassy golf course in the area? You and I know that said hotel is still paying the same for their power and other utilities, so what gives them the idea that they can up the cost of a night's stay? Yeah, I know—supply and demand! What really amazes me is the brainwashing that these hotel guests seem to have had. They all know that the prices are jacked up beyond reason for these few days, but they happily, and with no malice aforethought, go right ahead and book for the next year at the inflated price! Same as air travel. The plane fills up with passengers and flies from point A to point B, all things being equal, with the passenger paying x hundred dollars. Now—same plane, same passenger load, same route, but a change of date, and the price spirals. The plane still travels at the same speed, still employs the same number of service personnel, still consumes the same amount of fuel, but because it is now Thanksgiving/Christmas/spring break, the fare is doubled/tripled/quadrupled.

This is why I have never understood why it costs more to travel on the weekend. One would think it would cost less because most people who work during the week have more time to travel on weekends, and therefore the planes would be full. But let me tell you, gentle reader, that this is not the case! Want to fly on the weekend? That's prime travel time, for which we are going to make you pay through the nose! It may well be the law of supply and demand, but to my obviously non-economically trained brain, it's just wrong.

I am sure that if any economists are bored enough to take the time to read this rant, they will be laughing cynically and giving pitying looks to anyone who cares to observe them. This probably explains why I never seem to get ahead financially. My demand is high, but the supply seems a little lacking these days. What am I doing wrong, people? I'm certainly not putting ice in my tea—that's a given!

Jingle Tills, Jingle Tills!

I am delighted to be able to inform you all that on the 26th of December, the next official Christmas season will begin again. Instead of having a season from mid-July through December 25, why not start the whole season over again on December 26? I have officially seen reindeer with Easter baskets; really, I have. I do know that I saw a portly figure wearing red, white, and blue shorts brandishing candy canes on the 4th of July. He didn't actually say "Ho-ho-ho," but he looked as if he were about to. I have it on the best authority that Santa is no longer going to be a December snowbird; he is relocating permanently to the beach and may well switch his allegiance from penguins and elves to flamingoes and spring-breakers.

All of you up north have had more than your fair share of St. Nick, so now it's our turn. Whether Santa leaves the North Pole and flies south or gets off his beach towel and jogs north should not affect the outcome. It's silly to expect the jolly old gentleman to get all his deliveries out in one night, and we down here in the South have been campaigning for years to get this season recognized as an all-year event. Decorations for yards, houses, palm trees, Christmas trees, and even cars have been out in full force for ages. In fact, I don't think they ever left the store shelves. Many of us will join the ranks of the demented *after* Christmas to take advantage of the special sale prices, so that tills may continue to jingle. Also, there would be no need for Black Friday anymore. Those shopaholics can camp out all year round instead of just a couple of days during Thanksgiving. Let's spread the wealth, folks. This way, if you miss a bargain, go home and have a cuppa because there'll be another sale and another one and … get my meaning?

Just think! All those letters to Santa that flood the mail service during December would now be spread throughout the whole year, making it easier for Santa to get them read. This will take the pressure off him so that he can take his time getting presents wrapped and delivered to the nice ones, and the naughty ones can have a whole year to think about changing their ways instead of just a couple of weeks. So "Tis the Season to Be Jolly" could be sung all year round, along with "Jingle Tills."

About the Author

Valerie Crowe is a published author of children's stories, and she is now sharing some of her more amusing experiences as a recent newcomer to the United States with the adult market. While continuing to write, Crowe enjoys a busy retirement in Palm Harbor, Florida. She is the author of the Adventures of the Precious Knights Series.

Printed in the United States
By Bookmasters